Leisure Arts 34
Painting
Still Life in
Acrylics
Ray Campbell Smith

SEARCH PRESS

Introduction

The term 'still life' is used loosely to denote groups of objects either natural or man-made, or a combination of both. It can include such natural objects as flowers, fruit, or sea shells and range from artifacts such as fine glass and porcelain on the one hand to humble kitchen utensils on the other. The only criterion is the artistic appeal of the grouped objects—does their form, colour and texture produce a pleasing design? The intrinsic value of the objects may have little bearing on this question, for throughout the ages artists have delighted in painting everyday objects and in trying to bring to them a touch of magic and permanence. Such objects may form the centrepiece of a still life painting or may fill the humbler role of props in portrait or landscape paintings. In this book I shall be discussing still life as an end in itself.

Flower and plant painting is a separate and attractive branch of still life and I shall be devoting a section to it later in the book, (see pages 12–13). First, however, I shall consider groups of objects and suggest how to get the best out of them.

It makes good sense to group objects which bear some relation to each other and are not just a random collection of articles: this will give your painting point and a motive. Even more important is the need to include objects which, when carefully arranged, will produce a satisfying and balanced design, although some sort of connecting link between them will give the painting added interest. This careful arrangement, or composition, is fundamental to the success of still life work and is discussed in more detail on pages 10 and 11. For the present, suffice it to say that the objects should be so arranged that they relate to one another, perhaps by overlapping or by being connected by shadows.

Tonal contrast is also important, and is obtained by placing light objects against dark. Above all, the arrangement should have a feeling of balance so that, for instance, the weight and the interest are not all on one side. There is always the danger, however, that meticulous attention to considerations of composition may produce a somewhat contrived and artificial result, so, at the risk of seeming contradictory, try and make a conscious effort to retain spontaneity.

Materials

Although acrylic paints are a comparatively recent development, they have grown rapidly in popularity and their sales are constantly increasing. Their success stems directly from their unique properties which have satisfied a need long felt by artists. To begin with, they are water-based, which enables brushes and mixing palettes to be washed under the tap and obviates the need for strong smelling solvents. They are versatile in that they can be used straight from the tube to give an effect similar to oil paint, or they can be diluted with water to produce washes which look just like watercolour. Between these two extremes are many variations and it is these that give acrylics their individual character. Another useful property of acrylics is that of rapid drying; this enables further paint to be added without the long delay required by oils or the risk of disturbing the underpainting. The same is true of glazes which can be applied in fairly rapid succession to obtain interesting effects, such as subtle variations in the tone and colour of the underlying painting.

If you have not used acrylics before, this quick-drying characteristic can present problems. You may find that the drying process begins before you are ready for it and of course this applies with added force if you are painting in hot, dry conditions. The paint on your mixing palette can also dry prematurely and it is all too easy for particles of dry paint to become mixed with more liquid paint, to the detriment of the texture of the finished work. One of the solutions to this problem is more rapid work which might well impart greater freshness and punch to your painting; another is the use of a water spray and a retarding agent. When I am working in quick-drying conditions, I usually mix more water with my paint and periodically give my mixing palette a quick squirt from an adapted scent spray. One firm of art suppliers has evolved its own solution in the form of a 'Stay Wet' palette for acrylic paints.

When dry, acrylics become impervious to water so that you cannot 'lift out' small areas with a damp brush, as you can with watercolour. On drying, the paint forms a tough, rubbery film which is resistant to fading, cracking and crazing.

It is worth noting that, unlike watercolour, the paint

From top to bottom: sable brush, hog-hair brushes, acrylic tubes, and mixing palette.

darkens perceptibly as it dries and allowance has to be made for this.

There are a number of products on the market for mixing with acrylic paint, but I have never felt the need for these. When dry, acrylic paintings may be protected with either matt or gloss varnish, or with a mixture of the two.

A limited palette is always good practice and my normal range consists of ultramarine, Winsor blue, raw sienna, burnt sienna, light red, Payne's grey and titanium white. For flower painting, however, additional colours may well be required to produce those lovely glowing mauves, pinks, reds, oranges and yellows. I generally prefer a white plastic mixing surface when mixing paints, though I sometimes use a tear-off paper palette.

Unless you only intend to use acrylics like watercolour and apply the paint in liquid washes, you will need hogs-hair bristle brushes, with perhaps a small sable brush for detailed work. A word of warning here: it is vital that you wash your brushes promptly and thoroughly after use, or a rubbery deposit will build up at the base of the bristles and cause damage.

Almost any non-greasy surface is suitable for acrylics — canvas, paper, hardboard, card — and porous materials can be sealed with acrylic gesso primer to produce a good white painting surface.

3

Stage 1

Stage 2

Copper kettle: demonstration

Original size; 195mm × 250mm (7¾in × 10in)
Paper: Arches 300lb rough
Brushes: Bristle nos 7, 9. Sable nos 6, 8

Polished copper is an appealing subject for the still-life painter. This old kettle stands by my own fireside, though its object is decorative rather than functional and the same is true of the warming pan hanging on the wall. Together with the wrought iron of the poker, trivet and grate they form a pleasing group by the corner of the hearth, with warm colour and strong tonal contrast.

As the patina of light and shade on the copper was crisp and well-defined, I felt this could best be captured by using liquid washes of acrylic paint rather in the manner of watercolour. This treatment contrasts effectively with the rougher, more solid handling of the old brickwork and logs.

Stage 1

I begin by sketching in the positions of the principal objects of the group, using a small sable brush and dilute burnt sienna. Then I block-in the large area of shadowed brickwork, using burnt sienna, light red, ultramarine and a little titanium white, in order to define the dominant shapes of the composition.

Stage 2

I add the brickwork of the fire recess using a lighter, warmer version of the same mix, leaving a broken edge to accommodate the flames, which are then roughly indicated using raw and burnt sienna. I put in the brick courses with darker paint, keeping the brush strokes fairly rough to suggest old brickwork and avoid anything too tight which might suggest more regular, modern masonry. The fire-lit stone of the floor comes in next with raw and burnt sienna and shadows of light red and ultramarine, all with varying amounts of titanium white. The polished copper is rendered mainly in burnt sienna with light red and ultramarine in varying proportions for the shadows and dark reflections; but I take care to preserve the highlights and keep the treatment crisp.

Stage 3 – the finished painting

Stage 3 — the finished painting

The logs are tackled next with a mixture of raw and burnt sienna, ultramarine and white to give a warm khaki colour. Light red and ultramarine are mixed for the shadowed areas and are applied, dry brush fashion, to indicate the rough texture of the bark. The sawn edges are shown by pale shades of tan and grey and the radial splits in deeper tones. A few final touches and the painting is complete.

Draughtsmanship and perspective

The basis of all art is sound drawing for, however brilliant the painting technique, the finished work will only be as good as the underlying draughtsmanship. Of course, subjects differ widely in the demands they make upon drawing skill and a simple landscape of fields and trees will present far fewer problems than, for example, a group of figures against a complex background. But weak drawing, even of simple subjects, is difficult to hide and any painter who wishes to raise his or her standards should make a firm commitment to improving skill with the pencil.

There are no short cuts on this journey, but there are signposts for those prepared to look for them which may prevent many a wrong turning. The best advice consists of just two words — observe and practise. First, observe carefully and thoroughly the objects you are drawing and do not rest content with a cursory glance. Observe too, whenever you can, the work of accomplished artists and study how they tackle their subjects. Second, put in all the practice you can and let your sketchbook be your constant companion.

Perspective

Perspective is a subject which causes a great deal of needless difficulty. I say 'needless' because, once the comparatively simple rules are mastered, the problem ceases to be a problem!

These rules are based on the self-evident proposition that the further away an object is, the smaller it will appear, and when it is on the true horizon, it will virtually disappear. This is shown diagrammatically in Figure 1, below.

This diagram can be adapted to show how to construct the lines of a solid figure, such as the rectangular building shown in Figure 2. Notice that the lines above eye-level slope down to the disappearing point, while those below eye-level slope up to it, which, of course, accords with our observation. Notice too, that the true

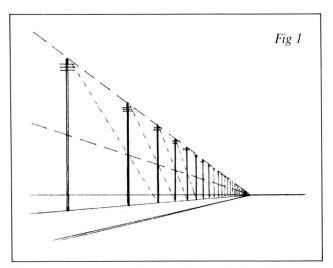

The further away an object is, the smaller it will appear.

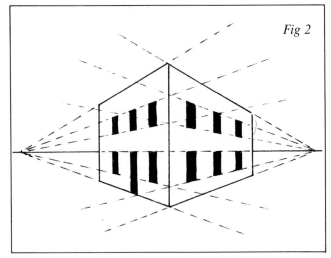

The lines above eye-level slope down to the disappearing point, those above slope up.

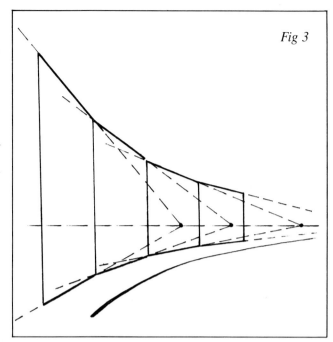

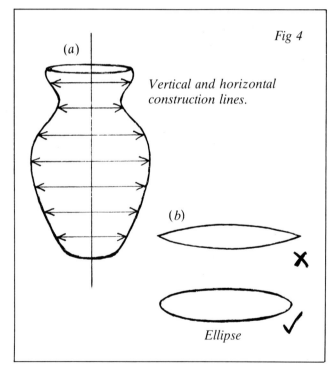

Fig 3

The position of disappearing points varies with the angle of the object.

in still-life groups, can cause the inexperienced artist difficulty. Figure 4 indicates (a) how symmetry may be obtained by the use of vertical and horizontal construction lines and (b) how the common fault of a torpedo-shaped ellipse may be avoided.

To draw a symmetrical vase like the one shown in (a) first construct a vertical line and then a series of lines, having equal length on either side of it and at right angles to it. The extremities of these lines, when joined, will give you the right and left-hand profiles of the vase. When drawing an ellipse as in (b), remember that it is simply a foreshortened circle and, although the curves at the right and left-hand extremities of a shallow ellipse will be very tight, they will not be sharp points.

Fig 4

(a)

Vertical and horizontal construction lines.

(b)

Ellipse

horizon is synonymous with eye-level and is often, in practice, obscured by hills or other nearer features. Only the sea horizon, or the horizon of a dead level plain, will coincide with the true horizon.

The nearer an object is, the steeper will be the perspective slope. Another point to note is that the position of the disappearing points will vary with the angle of the object, which Figure 3, showing a curving line of houses, makes clear.

It is, of course, possible to use these methods to construct your objects, but it is probably better to use them to check what you have drawn against perspective error.

Earthenware vessels and china vases, frequently seen

Tone

In the language of art, tone refers to the relative lightness and darkness of objects but not, as in common parlance, to their colour. The success of a painting depends largely on the correctness of its tone values yet, despite this, painters who give long and careful consideration to colour sometimes pay scant attention to tone. However, if the tone values of a painting are correct, that painting will stand up just as well if photographed in black and white.

If you have difficulty in evaluating correct tones, it may help if you identify the lightest and the darkest tones in your composition, and establish these first. The half dozen or so intermediate tones may then be arranged within these two extremes. Difficulty often arises when the darkest paint is used on objects which are not at the bottom of the tonal scale, for there is then nothing in reserve for even darker objects.

In this context still life has one big advantage over landscape painting: for it is a comparatively simple matter to control the amount and the direction of the light falling upon the subject in a way the landscape painter may well envy. The composition can be so arranged that the highlights and shadows fall where required, thus enabling tonal contrast to be accentuated. By the same token light objects may be placed against dark, with the same objective in view.

Since acrylic paint darkens appreciably on drying, it is all too easy to allow this to upset tone values. Fortunately with acrylics lighter paint may be added to raise tone without any loss of freshness.

In the painting of vegetables shown opposite, some of the principles I have mentioned have been put into effect. There is, for example, an overall tonal balance and plenty of tonal contrast. The lightest lights — the corner of the window and the highlights on some of the vegetables — are at the top of the tonal scale and almost white. At the bottom of this scale are the deep shadows cast by the objects and by the surface on which they rest. In between these extremes is the range of intermediate tones which helps to describe the form of the group.

In planning this arrangement, I kept constantly in mind the desirability of placing light objects against dark to obtain what is known as 'counterchange', and you will notice how the pale tones of the cabbage and the trug have been set against the dark background. The foreground vegetables, too, make a pale accent against the shadowed side of the trug.

Fig 5

Fig 6

Fig 7

Fig 8

Composition

One of the problems facing the landscape painter is that of finding a satisfactory composition. It is not a difficult matter to find subjects that are attractive in themselves, but the painter needs more than this — he needs a subject in which there is balance and harmony. The problem can usually be overcome by careful reconnaissance which aims to find a vantage point from which the elements of the scene will arrange themselves in a balanced manner. Occasionally, however, one comes across a scene which refuses to respond to this treatment: all the artist can then do is to make the best of it or, in his imagination, vary the arrangement of the scene before him to improve its composition — a ploy that does not meet with universal approval. The still-life painter has no such difficulty, for he can arrange his subject-matter at will until he is satisfied with the resulting composition.

So far I have begged the basic question, 'what is good composition?' One can, of course, say that in a good composition there is a balance and a harmony about the arrangement that is pleasing, but a less vague approach is to list the various pitfalls to avoid.

The most obvious fault is that of placing a dominant object right in the middle of the painting — much better to place it a bit off centre and balance it with something else, (see Figure 5). Similarly, a dominant line, such as the edge of a supporting table, should not cut straight across the middle of the paper, (see Figure 6). Nor should the objects in a still-life painting be placed in a row — Figure 7 shows how much more pleasing the arrangement will look if the objects are grouped, with some overlapping. The objects need not all overlap, but it helps if there is some connecting link such as a horizontal shadow.

In drawing a group of objects one should always be aware of the position of the margins of the paper or canvas, for these lines have an important part to play in the overall composition of which they are a part. The space around and between the objects is important and the temptation to cram too much on to the paper should be firmly resisted.

Another important consideration is that of tonal balance. The group should not be so arranged that all the tonal weight is on one side. In this context, background tone can be used to effect an acceptable balance, as Figure 8 illustrates. One should also seek to place light objects against dark, to obtain counterchange, (this is explained on page 8 in the section on tone) for this adds sparkle and interest to the arrangement.

It is worth reiterating that it is all too easy for the technically correct composition to look somewhat artificial and contrived while more informal arrangements can possess an agreeable spontaneity and freshness. So be on your guard against anything that is too conventional and stodgy. It is a good plan to keep an eye open for good natural compositions and record them in one's sketchbook. A collection of toys abandoned by children may have more to offer than a tight, formal grouping. It is also worthwhile to make sketches of several alternative arrangements of still-life objects for the most pleasing sketch will probably make the best painting.

When you sketch a still-life arrangement, experiment with differing viewpoints, for an unconventional slant can often add interest and originality to a group of mundane objects.

Plant: demonstration

Original size: 250mm × 250mm (10in × 10in)
Paper: Arches 300lb rough
Brushes: Sable nos 8, 10, 12

The demonstration overleaf is a bold and direct treatment of a group of daisy-like blooms in a natural setting. The intention is to convey a strong impression of the flower-heads without too much labouring after exact form. To make the petals appear to shine, the background is tackled in deep, contrasting tones and detail of stalk and leaf is merely suggested. For this treatment I use acrylics as watercolours, employing no white and mixing my colours in clear, full washes.

Stage 1

Stage 2

Stage 1

I begin by lightly sketching in the approximate shapes and positions of the flower-heads and a few leaves, using a no.8 sable brush and a wash of weak ultramarine. The drawing is kept to a minimum because I want the later brush strokes to provide their own dynamic outlines to the blooms.

Stage 2

I now paint in the flower-heads with a no.10 sable brush, using very liquid washes of colour, with no added white, thus ensuring freshness, clarity and translucence. The white blooms are painted with very pale washes of green and yellow, the pink with a mixture of vermilion and alizarin and the mauve with a wash of ultramarine plus a touch of alizarin. The leaves are a clear wash of Winsor blue and raw sienna, warmed here and there with a little burnt sienna. Slightly deeper accents of the same mixtures are applied here and there to suggest the forms of the petals and leaves.

Stage 3 — the finished painting

I continue the process of painting in the deep, greenish background, working quickly and boldly with full washes of rich colour mixed in advance. For this I use a no.12 sable brush and four wells of mixed colour. These washes are: (a) ultramarine, alizarin and light red; (b) Winsor blue and raw sienna; (c) Payne's grey; and (d) burnt sienna. These strong but liquid colours blend and, while they are still wet, I add darker accents to suggest shadows. I add a few more bold touches to the blooms and the leaves, to create form. I finally add a few darker brush strokes to the background and firmly resist the temptation to elaborate further.

Stage 3 – the finished painting

Texture

Painters are not only concerned with the tone and colour of their subjects but need to convey their texture as well. This is particularly true of the still-life painter, for the textures of the objects he paints—some natural, some man-made, vary enormously. Porcelain, polished wood and metal, for example, all have their own individual gloss while glass presents a unique problem — for not only its shine but its transparency too must be faithfully portrayed. Pay particular attention to its refractive properties and note the distortion of image they produce.

At the other end of the scale are such matt materials as unglazed earthenware and unpolished wood while, between the two extremes, is a whole range of differing textures, each presenting its challenge to the painter's skill and resource. As with so much in art, the starting-point must be thorough observation and careful analysis of the surface textures. With glossy materials there must often be some simplification to avoid giving an impression of fussy over-elaboration. It is possible to eliminate much of this problem and ensure, by the careful arrangement of objects, that there is not too much fiddly detail for the shiny surfaces to reflect.

Matt surfaces present an entirely different problem: they reflect very little, although of course even the dullest surface is responsive to reflected light and colour. Careful attention to reflected light will help to impart a three dimensional quality and add a glow to the shadows.

Acrylic paint is a splendid medium for portraying texture for it lends itself well to a number of techniques that can be employed to produce differing effects, (see below). A rough surface can be represented by a scumbling technique, or by the dry-brush application of a lighter tone over a darker background. Successive glazes of thin paint will produce interesting and useful effects while, at the other extreme, heavy impasto work is good for portraying rough plaster or stucco. Painting knives can produce crisp, faceted marks to represent effectively such subjects as foliage and tree bark. In addition to the textured effects below there are many other possibilities. Have a go yourself and see what you can produce with a hog-hair brush, sable brush, painting knife, or even an index finger. You will find it a fascinating exercise and one that will stand you in good stead in all your still-life work.

Light texturing over darker paint

Palette knife impasto

Dark glaze over lighter paint

Painting dark to light

Dry brush work on rough surface

Clear liquid wash

Studio window

This is an impression of the window of my studio. In reality it faces north, in the approved manner — for the north provides the most consistent light with no danger of direct sun — but I have taken liberties with the points of the compass in order to introduce some sunshine and shadow into the room. I felt that an oblique viewpoint would be preferable to a four-square arrangement and would produce a more balanced and satisfying composition.

The treatment of the view through the window has been kept light in order to contrast with the deeper tones of the interior. The window frames present a dark accent against the pale sky and the heavy blue curtains contrast with and frame the lighter area between. At first I cleared the table top, but it then seemed a little lifeless and, as it is usually cluttered, I decided that tidying up was not such a good idea, even though I did not want to have too much detail in the foreground.

This composition is really an exercise in providing a meaningful setting for a group of still-life objects. There is just enough detail in the exterior view to provide interest, but not enough to compete with the foreground. With all subjects, particularly those containing a window, a conscious decision has to be made about the nature and position of the centre of interest. It could well be the view through the window, in which case the foreground would be simplified and played down; or it could equally be the still-life objects inside, as in this instance, with the exterior view understated. A painting in which the interior and the exterior are given equal prominence is usually unsatisfactory because it leaves the eye in limbo.

Light

The quality of the light falling on a landscape fundamentally affects the appearance of the scene and hence the artist's response to it. With still-life subjects the quality of the light is no less important although it may often be modified and controlled during the arrangement of the subject-matter. With a collection of three-dimensional objects an oblique light will help to emphasize form and shape while the shadows themselves constitute an integral part of the composition.

As well as delineating form and improving compositional balance, light has an important part to play in helping to establish atmosphere. If you compare the Mediterranean scene on page 29 with the more shadowy painting opposite, you will see how the one engenders a sunny, holiday mood, but the other produces a more sombre, reflective and introspective atmosphere. In the latter case, the single subdued light barely penetrates the surrounding gloom and focuses attention on the book and the spectacles, to produce a feeling of studious isolation from the outside world.

Though it is simple, there is a balance and a unity about this composition which is analysed in the diagram, or composition analysis, on this page. A successful composition usually resolves into a series of shapes which make up a pleasing pattern. The lines that form the margin of paper or canvas are a vital part of this overall design and have also to be taken into account when the composition is being planned. Here the light area of the lampshade is balanced by the pale pages of the open book and the two are connected by the oblique area of radiance. The rectangle of standing books balances and contrasts with the circular form of the table lamp base, while the spaces between the various objects form interesting shapes in their own right. The gleams of light on the spectacles and on the top of the lamp base impart a spark of life to the painting.

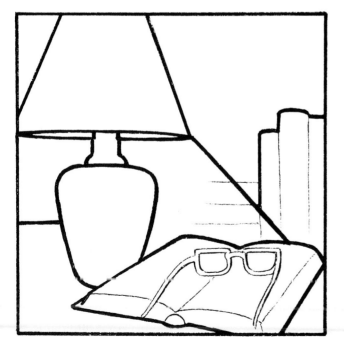

Kitchen table: demonstration

Original size: 250mm × 250mm (10in × 10in)
Canvas: Fine grain canvas
Brushes: Bristle nos 8, 10. Sable nos 6, 8

The demonstration overleaf is a collection of work-a-day objects which one might see on any kitchen table, but grouped together they provide a pleasing overall composition at the same time as giving rise to a variety of interesting shapes. The slightly oblique angle of the table and the contrasting tone and colour of background and surface contribute to the overall design. Because the arrangement is fairly complex, the wall and table surface have been treated as flat planes of colour.

Stage 1

Stage 2

Stage 1

I sketch the objects in burnt sienna and, simultaneously, emphasise the shapes of the space between and around them. At this stage it is comparatively easy to judge the effectiveness or otherwise of the overall design, and weaknesses reveal themselves clearly. Here the design calls for an additional feature to break up the expanse of green and provide balance, so a small window is added at the top right of the painting.

For the subdued green of the background wall I use a combination of ultramarine, Payne's grey and raw sienna, plus titanium white.

Stage 2

The scrubbed wood of the kitchen table calls for raw sienna and titanium white. To provide counterchange, I emphasize the shadow beneath the table, and this also strengthens the shape of the foreground chair. The various touches of vermilion, complementary to the

expanse of green, help to lift the painting and give it life, rather as a small red figure in a predominantly green setting adds point to a landscape.

The earthenware pitcher is rendered mainly in light red with a little ultramarine.

Stage 3 — the finished painting

I tackle next the shiny metal objects, for which I use fairly liquid washes of ultramarine plus a little light red, leaving the untouched white canvas to stand for the highlights. The polished metal reflects a super-abundance of detail which needs considerable simplification. The dark green bottle, the jar of preserves and the shadows falling across the table all require further attention and the pitcher needs enlivening with burnt sienna.

Stage 3 – the finished painting

Backgrounds and surfaces

In one's eagerness to arrange a group of objects in an attractive and satisfying manner, it is all too easy to pay too little attention to background and surface. Both, however, have a vital part to play in a successful composition.

First, the surface upon which the chosen group of objects stands. This will usually be a table with, perhaps, some form of covering. I have already mentioned, in the section on composition, (see pages 10 and 11), that an important construction line, such as the edge of a table, should not cut horizontally across the centre of paper or canvas. In all probability this line will be in the lower half of the painting to allow sufficient space for the objects resting upon it. If it is drawn at a slight angle to the top and bottom margins of the support, so much the better.

The second consideration is the table covering. Here much depends on the nature of the still-life articles: if they are complicated in form and colour, a fairly plain fabric should be chosen so as not to compete with the complexities of the objects above it. Alternatively, it could be decided that no covering at all is necessary, although not, probably, if the table is so highly polished that it produces anything approaching a mirror image. With simple objects, patterned materials are perfectly suitable, though care should be taken to ensure their perspective is in harmony with that of the surface on which they stand — not always easy with complex designs.

Tone is another consideration to be borne in mind, for tonal contrast is vital to the success of any still-life painting. If the objects are light in tone — for example a white porcelain tea set — they will show up better against a dark surface and background. The reverse will apply, of course, if the objects are predominantly dark. If, as is more likely, the group consists of a mixture of light and dark objects, not only should the light be placed against the dark to provide counterchange, but the background and the lighting should be so arranged that here, too, there is tonal contrast.

Curtains and other drapes are often used to provide backgrounds for still-life arrangements. These can be perfectly satisfactory, if somewhat conventional, but it is worth considering alternatives. One often sees still-life paintings in which the backgrounds are just areas of tone and colour, suitable for setting off the objects in front of them, but without any particular meaning. Admittedly, the background should not be so definite that it competes with the still-life arrangement, but in my view it should represent something tangible, otherwise the setting becomes somewhat artificial. This accords with the objective of making still-life arrangements appear both natural and spontaneous.

It is good therapy for the still-life painter to get away periodically from conventional subjects and look for something entirely new. This search need not be confined to the house. Tennis racquets, balls and white sweaters draped negligently over canvas chairs, for example, might make an appealing subject in a leafy garden setting. A group of skis, and gaily coloured anoraks against a snowy backdrop of mountains could offer an evocative and dramatic painting.

In the sketch opposite I have taken as my subject the nautical clutter inseparable from the vicinity of fishermen's huts. I came across the scene quite by chance and immediately recognised a natural composition full of character and unusual shapes. The beamy old wooden-hulled fishing boat, the sleeker plastic covered dinghy hull, the ramshackle huts and the assortment of masts, provide a fit setting for the still-life objects in the foreground.

I worked rapidly and loosely, using watercolour brushes with liquid washes which dried rapidly in the warm breeze. I emphasized line here and there with a fountain pen filled with black ink. This use of acrylics, rather in the manner of line and wash, is far removed from the more usual oil-painting approach and shows how versatile this medium can be. With quick-drying washes you simply have to work rapidly, and with the right subject this can give added spontaneity and vigour to your work.

Colour

In writing about art materials, (see pages 2 and 3), I mentioned the advantages of using a limited palette, for harmony of colour and unity of composition are both served by using a small number of tubes. As our painting experience grows, we usually find we can dispense with certain colours on which we had previously relied, and can mix the subtlest shades from our 'basics'. In this we are following the example of many old masters, notably Rembrandt.

Choice of colour is a personal matter and most artists evolve a range which suits their particular style and needs. In so doing they add an individual quality which makes their work easy to identify. I personally have reduced my range over the years to just six, plus of course, titanium white. Ultramarine, Winsor blue, raw sienna, burnt sienna, light red and Payne's grey give me all I find I need for landscape work, though there is nothing sacred, of course, about this particular range. Still life is another matter; painting flowers, and to a lesser extent fruit, calls for a wider palette which will enable us to mix vibrant reds, oranges, yellows, pinks and purples. Some brightly coloured man-made objects, such as children's toys, may also require stronger and brighter colours than one's basic palette and so additions have to be made.

The fact that acrylic paints darken on drying poses problems for artists accustomed to watercolours, which do the reverse, and it takes some getting used to. Unless allowance is made for this, however, paintings will end up looking uniformly dingy. On the contrary, you should strive to give your work liveliness and punch by emphasizing contrast in both tone and colour. I have mentioned the advantage of placing lights against darks, but you can also strengthen the colours you wish to emphasize by putting complementary colours against them. Complementary colours are opposites — red and green, blue and yellow, for example. You can make a colour glow by surrounding it with a darker shade of its complementary.

You may have noticed that there is no black in my palette. This does not mean I feel no need on occasion for dark shadows because it is possible to obtain deep tones by, for example, mixing ultramarine and burnt sienna. By avoiding black, which is a dead colour, and using deep mixes of other colours, shadows can be painted that are deep yet vibrant with life. Always look for reflected light in your shadows, for they add a glow and a richness to dark areas. One side of a sunny street may be in deep shadow but the light reflected from the sunny side will add immensely to its interest. The same applies to the shadows in a still-life arrangement and you should always be alert to recognize reflected colour as, for instance, when the warm glow of an orange modifies the colour of the pale cloth on which it is standing.

Above all, look for hues other than the obvious and expected ones. This analytical approach has to be cultivated and conventions put on one side. To young children, tree foliage is uniformly green and tree trunks are chocolate brown and this is how they paint them. The artist will see yellows, oranges and browns in foliage and his painting will reflect this, giving his work variety, richness and, indeed, truth.

Opposite: the colours of the fruit offer a lively contrast to the dark background.

The importance of shadows

In the section on 'Light' (see page 18), I indicated how shadows, and the interplay of light and shade, delineate the form and substance of the chosen composition. Here I want to discuss the treatment of shadows themselves, and there is, of course, a strong link with the earlier sections on 'Tone' and 'Colour' (pages 8 and 24 respectively). This may at first sight seem confusing but, in painting, light, shade, tone and colour are all interrelated. This must constantly be borne in mind, even though, for the purpose of analysis, they are often treated separately.

Always the darkest paint must be reserved for the deepest shadows and the tones of the lighter shadows carefully assessed. A common fault is that we often give all the shadows virtually the same tone value, thereby robbing the painting of power, vitality and mystery. Shadow tones will vary, depending on their position vis-a-vis the light source and also by virtue of the tone of the surface on which they fall. In addition there are usually tonal variations within the individual shadow, with the deepest near the centre base of the object casting the shadow and the lightest at the shadow margins. There will often be reflected light on the shadowed side of the object itself and this too needs to be given careful attention.

Another common fault of many artists is, as I have said, that of failing to do justice to the rich, if subdued, colours contained in many shadows. They are frequently modified by the colours of adjoining objects, particularly those in full light and which are strongly coloured.

Such surfaces as polished metal and glass readily reflect light, while opaque and matt materials tend to absorb it. By faithfully depicting the amount and the quality of the light and shade reflected, it is easy to indicate the nature of the material being painted. In the painting opposite, the reflective qualities of polished metal and of unpolished wood are clearly contrasted. Note, too, the difference in tone between the shadows on the workbench and the deep shadow beneath it.

As with so much in art, the key is careful observation. To be able to convey a vivid and powerful image, it is necessary to study, to analyse, to assimilate, and to feel.

Above: shadows are reflected in a hammer and saw.

Opposite: note the difference in tone between the shadows on top of the workbench and the deep shadow beneath it.

Stage 1

Stage 2

Cretan patio: demonstration

Original size: 250mm × 250mm (10in × 10in)
Canvas: Fine grain canvas
Brushes: Bristle nos 8, 10. Sable no 8.

This painting of a Cretan patio, halfway between a still life and a landscape, shows how still-life objects play their part in a broader picture and add interest and immediacy to the whole scene.

Stage 1

I begin by sketching the scene in neat Vandyke brown, paying careful attention to the perspective which plays a vital role in the oblique composition. The time is mid-morning and the light clear and bright. If the light were of the warm evening variety I would begin with an overall wash of dilute raw sienna plus a little light red. As it is, I paint the sky, the distant hills and the sea directly on to the white canvas, using varying mixtures of ultramarine and light red, and ultramarine and raw sienna, plus titanium white. Touches of light red suggest the terracotta roofs.

Stage 2

I complete the middle-distance buildings, using raw sienna and titanium white for the sunlit stucco, and ultramarine, light red and titanium white for the shadowed walls. Payne's grey and raw sienna render the foliage, with added Payne's grey for the cypress trees.

When tackling the foreground, I allow traces of the brown construction lines to show through here and

Stage 3 – the finished painting

there, thus adding strength and providing contrast with the softer treatment of the more distant view. I then indicate carefully the warmth of reflected light in the shadowed areas of the foreground wall.

Stage 3

It now remains to paint in the foreground objects. The tablecloth is just white canvas, and its shadows are produced with pale ultramarine and light red. The tones and colours I use are designed to convey an impression of strong Mediterranean sunlight in which, of course, cast shadows have an important part to play. Lastly a

few flicks of white for the distant sails and the painting is complete.

When I had finished the painting, it seemed to me that the table looked somewhat sparse and the objects upon it rather unconnected. I therefore added a pannier of oranges, a stick of bread and an extra bottle of red wine. Not only do these additions serve to tie the objects together and provide a more harmonious group, but the vivid splash of orange helps to balance the bright colours in the other half of the painting. Second thoughts of this kind present no problems with acrylics for their covering power is such that you just paint over the top.

Holiday luggage

It is all too easy for the still-life painter to stick to convention and paint old books, polished copper, fruit, flowers and suchlike. There is nothing wrong with this as far as it goes, and it is nonsense to maintain, as some do, that an attractive subject is taboo simply because it has been painted many times before by other artists. All painters are individuals and most have something personal to say about any given subject. At the same time we should all be on the look-out for groups of objects, however unconventional, that will arrange themselves into interesting compositions.

The painting opposite was made from a quick sketch of a neighbour's car shortly before it was packed for a family holiday. It is not the sort of subject that normally attracts painters but to my mind it contains a number of unusual shapes, plenty of tonal contrast, and a variety of surface textures ranging from shiny chromium to worn leather. Technically the composition could have been improved by altering a little the positions of the suitcases, but equally this might well have made it appear somewhat contrived.

A composition of this kind lends itself to treatment in a more abstract fashion, with the accent on the interplay of shapes and colours, to produce a lively design. In the abstract study on this page the lines have been simplified with this object in view. Simplification can be carried even further so that all realism is lost and just a pattern remains, but my preference is for a design which is

recognisably based on real objects. In the last analysis, perhaps, it is a matter of personal interpretation and taste.

First published in Great Britain 1989 by Search Press Limited, Wellwood, North Farm Road, Tunbridge Wells, Kent TN2 3DR

Text, drawings and paintings by Ray Campbell Smith

Text, illustrations, arrangement and typography copyright © Search Press Limited 1989

U.S. Artists Materials Trade Distributors:
Winsor & Newton, Inc.
11 Constitution Avenue, P.O. Box 1396, Piscataway, NJ 08855-1396

Canadian Distributors:
Anthes Universal Limited
341 Heart Lake Road South, Brampton, Ontario L6W 3K8

Australian Distributors:
Jasco Pty Limited
937-941 Victoria Road, West Ryde, N.S.W. 2114

New Zealand Distributors:
Caldwell Wholesale Limited
Wellington and Auckland

ISBN 0 85532 633 6

Typeset by Scribe Design, 123 Watling Street, Gillingham, Kent Made and printed in Spain by A.G. Elkar S. Coop. Bilbao-12